Beloved,

Be Blessed in Jes 1:5

Thank You, JESUS!

Stephen Andrew Totin

Bro Steve

Copyright © 2009 by Stephen A. Totin
Published in The United States of America by
True Potential Publishing, Inc.
PO Box 904 Travelers Rest, SC 29690
http://tppress.com

All rights reserved.
No part of this publication may be reproduced or transmitted in any form or by any means, electronic or mechanical, including photocopy, recording or any information storage and retrieval system, without permission from the publisher.

ISBN 978-0-9823059-9-7

Library of Congress Control Number: 2009938590

Printed in the USA

Thank You, Jesus!

Stephen Andrew Totin

Preface

Allow me to share what ***Thank You, Jesus!*** is all about.

It is the true story of a young couple gifted by God Almighty.

Many years before they laid eyes on each other, God prepared them to cross paths. They fell in love in 1957. By October 1959, Dorothy and Steve graced the altar of St. Ignatius Polish Catholic Church in Glendale, Pennsylvania, and became man and wife in one spirit.

See how the Holy Spirit of God trained them to pray for others in need, even before the answers came, giving God all the praise and glory by uttering *"Thank You, Jesus!"*

Sit back and enjoy reading the wonderful testimonies that blossomed out of faith in their God.

Stephen A. Totin
Pittsburgh, Pennsylvania
February 2009

Foreword

Don't believe a word in this book! That's right! But believe ON THE WORD in this book as Brother Steve Totin reveals the secrets of faith heretofore kept hidden until this appointed time!

You will immediately witness the powerful, miraculous unfolding of a born-again life in Jesus Christ, as Steve believes, and shows you how his steps have been ordered and ordained by his Creator.

Steve's riveting account will capture your attention, as he challenges and encourages YOU to believe ON THE WORD!

Alan Jennings
Television Journalist/Reporter

TABLE OF CONTENTS

Chapter	Page
1. *Lord, My Healer*	1
2. *Thou Shalt Not Steal*	9
3. *The Peace That Passes All Understanding*	11
4. *First Love*	14
5. *My Protector*	16
6. *His Eye Is On the Sparrow, And I Know He Watches Me*	19
7. *Lean Not To Your Own Understanding*	22
8. *Angel Unaware*	26
9. *My Dorothy*	28
10. *Goodbye, City Life!*	32
11. *Don't Be Deceived*	35
12. *Fear Creates Havoc*	38
13. *God Knows My Thoughts ... Be My Witness*	42
14. *Through the Fire*	46
15. *Prayer Changes Situations*	49
16. *Prison Ministry*	52
17. *God Honors Obedience*	55
18. *Fear Not, I Am With You*	58
19. *No Weapon Formed Against Me Shall Prosper*	63
20. *All Things Are Possible With God*	67

21. *Cathy With A "C"*	69
22. *He Will Never Leave You Nor Forsake You*	72
23. *Perfect Love Casteth Out Fear*	77
Closing ... *For The Moment*	79
Comments	81

CHAPTER ONE

Lord, My Healer

Have you ever been ill for a long time, and the medication and rest just isn't doing anything? You've prayed, and been prayed for, with no results.

Years ago, I contracted a severe cold, a nagging cough, and soreness in the rib cage with pain whenever I coughed. Finally, I decided to visit the Veteran's Outpatient Clinic in Pittsburgh, Pennsylvania. It was a Friday morning, and I had a 7 a.m. appointment. A friend of mine who worked in the Outpatient Department said, "Come before 7 a.m., and I'll get you in and out quickly."

I was weak and felt awfully warm at times; nevertheless, I drove into downtown Pittsburgh for the examination. After some blood work and x-rays, the results were more serious than I had imagined. The diagnosis was pneumonia in the right lung and bronchitis. I was ordered back home to bed. "Gee whiz," I thought, "not more bed rest. That's what I've been doing for days." I was losing weight also; food had lost its taste. I walked out of the clinic at 7:50 a.m. I felt too weak even to walk the 5 ½ blocks to where I had finally found a parking lot.

I hadn't visited my parents throughout the ordeal. With

Thank You, Jesus!

dad employed at Gimbel's Department Store in the area, I decided to pay him a short visit. The distance from the Veteran's Clinic to the store was only about two blocks. I entered the store and saw my dad, who was always there for me and my sisters and brother. Dad saw me coming down the escalator and was beaming that famous smile of his. Feeling blessed to be his firstborn son, I quietly said, "Hi, dad." He was taken by surprise and asked why I was at the store so early. I said, "I've been to the VA for an examination." Dad and Mom knew that I wasn't feeling well because my wife, Dorothy, kept close tabs with Mom since both believed in prayer and were praying for me. "Well," he asked, "What did they say is wrong?" "Pneumonia in the right lung and bronchitis." He asked how I'd gotten downtown. I told him I'd driven myself. Dad asked if that was wise. I answered, "I don't really know or care, and besides, I hadn't anyone to bring me."

Being a service-connected status veteran with a formerly diseased liver that I contracted in Korea, I wanted a second opinion since I wasn't getting any better and thinking maybe the root of my sickness was a flare-up of the diseased liver ... but it wasn't.

"For what it's worth," Dad added, "across from the store, that First Presbyterian Church at this moment is having one of those healing services directed by Kathryn Kuhlman." I wasn't sure Dad even believed in this way of healing aside from medicine. I kind of laughed and said, "I don't think she's for real, Dad." "Well," he interjected, "it wouldn't hurt to go and see for yourself." I asked him when it started, and Dad answered, "9 a.m." He added, "I heard folks start coming by 6 a.m." I thought to myself, "Stupid people!" I told my Dad goodbye and headed home. I walked outside and saw the church. "Oh, what can I lose?" I thought. It sure looked empty outside. I crossed the street, walked up the steps, and gingerly opened the heavy oak door just to take a peek. Suddenly, an usher opened it fully and caught me off guard. I hesitated, not sure I wanted to enter. I wanted only a peek. "Just looking," I said. Of course, I didn't tell him I was somewhat scared and, at the same time, not feeling well enough to be bothered with any of them.

He asked, "Well, are you coming in or not?" I was ready to answer, "Hey, man, get off my back. Leave me alone!" Then—just like that—I was in the vestibule. I could hear music and, through the vestibule doors, I could see a lot of people. I didn't realize the enormous size of the place. Then this persistent man said, "Son, you can't stay here. Follow me, and I'll seat you." I found myself walking behind this man going directly into the main room with hundreds of people singing, *"How Great Thou Art."* "Where's he taking me?" I couldn't get his attention. "Hey, I don't like sitting up front. Get me a back seat." Not this usher; he was on a mission with me right behind him. Then this lady in a white gown is right there on the platform saying something weird. This guy walks up on the platform and seats me directly behind this woman in white. Sitting on a folding chair, I was embarrassed and could feel my blood pressure at its peak. Then, as quick as that, the usher disappeared. Have you ever felt like a fish out of water? That was me.

I felt like everybody was staring at this tall, lanky man coming in late and distracting their service. "My God," I thought, "why did I follow him? I don't even believe in these services, and that lady is kind of spooky." Truly, I

Thank You, Jesus!

wasn't paying too much attention to what she was saying as she moved quickly up onto the platform.

I felt light headed as behind me sat a few elderly African-American women who every so often would say, "Thank You, Jesus"—kind of noisily, too.

Then the lady in white went off of the platform saying, "God is healing backs and spines." From where I was sitting, I couldn't see too much. I just heard her and a lot of noisy folks saying, "I'm free of pain" and "I feel so good"—folks laughing and clapping and praising God. I thought, "Oh, yeah, that's what you say"—but actually I was making fun of them. And this lady Ms. Kuhlman—so sad what people would believe.

Suddenly, Ms. Kuhlman came back up on the platform and looked my way and said, "There's a person in this area that has been suffering from a severe infection in their lungs, and God is healing you right now."

I was shocked, embarrassed to claim it only because of being so proud. I wasn't about to be knocked to the floor as I witnessed others who were saying, "God healed me." Does she push them down? "Not me," I thought, "not me. I'm not going down." I didn't claim it was me. One of the black ladies behind me got hysterical and started shouting, "It's me, Lord. It's me." Ms. Kuhlman said, "It's not you. It's a man, dearie."

Would you believe I sat there until 1 p.m.? Finally, I stood up, somewhat starved and confused. Maybe I should have said, "It's me, it's me," but I didn't. I wondered if God was mad at me, so I drove home and couldn't wait to lie down. I was drained of strength. About 20 minutes after I arrived home, my phone rang. It was my sister, Evelyn. "Steve, my God, what were you doing in the Kathryn Kuhlman service this morning?" We all saw you, and Steve, God was calling you—that healing of the lung was for you. "Yes," I said, "I goofed. I was too proud." Evelyn said, "Well, next meeting, I'm going to come with you, and we'll sit together." "No way am I going at 6 a.m. You go, Evelyn, and I'll meet you if you save me a seat." "Okay," she replied, "I'll call you later," and hung up.

Well, it's another Friday Ms. Kuhlman service. As promised, Evelyn saved me a seat. It was 8:50 a.m., and the excitement was already in bloom. I was seated about fifteen rows from the front.

The organ sounded, and the worship started. The air was electrified. The anointing was already there. Ms. Kuhlman stepped onto the platform. God had sent His servant to minister to His people once again. The congregation burst into thunderous applause—a spontaneous demonstration of their love for her. The ovation ceased abruptly as she led the crowd of standing people in her theme song:

"He touched me, Oh, He touched me,
And oh, the joy that floods my soul.
Something happened and now I know
He touched me—and made me whole."

God was smiling as she sang it once, twice—and over and over. Everyone was singing; all had hands raised to their Savior. Chills raced through my body. My hair and my body tingled. Kathryn came down off the platform with that glorious smile as the music continued. The Healer was in the church, and Ms. Kuhlman knew it wasn't

Thank You, Jesus!

her. The Anointed One with the nail-scarred hands was going through the pews, touching and healing whosoever. At times, Kathryn never said a word. Then, suddenly, she would call out, "God is healing a bad heart" or "healing a cancerous tumor." "A blind eye is seeing for the first time." On and on, she would call out what she heard God say to her, and people would see and feel His power go through them in a split second. Praise would be offered up all over the sanctuary. Then, Ms. Kuhlman stopped at my row and said, "God is healing a man of an infected lung and respiratory condition." "Well," Evelyn says, "It's my brother, it's my brother," and takes my right hand and lifts it up. Kathryn says, "Bring him out." I'm about thirteen seats into the row. Everyone's looking at me to come out. I hesitate, but Evelyn pushes me; I feel nothing in my body. Everyone is excited. I'm not one hundred percent sure. Kathryn moves quickly back up to the platform while Evelyn and I are making our way up front where we are met by a medical doctor who is asking me about my problem. I tell him that I've had pneumonia and bronchitis for eighty-seven days, right lung. He places the stethoscope on my chest telling me to breathe deeply; I won't do it because it hurts so badly. He assures me I should try anyway. I'm afraid, hesitant, knowing the pain is always there.

Ms. Kuhlman starts down the platform steps and says, "The Holy Spirit is all over you. God is healing you right now," with her hand stretched out to me some five or six feet away. No one touched me, at least no earthly vessel. Suddenly, I'm on the floor along with Evelyn, trying to get up but I can't. My legs aren't working. I try again and tumble almost on my head. Yet there is no one near me other than Evelyn, and she can't help herself, let alone me.

Lord, My Healer

This is known, in the Bible, as "slain in the Spirit."

The entire congregation is clapping, praising God, and I start to laugh. I feel peaceful and finally I'm able to sit upright, still on the floor. Something's wrong. I feel different. I feel light. No more pride. Ms. Kuhlman walked over with two large ushers who lift me up. I'm not too sure I can stand by myself. She says, "Well, well, how do we feel now?" I'm not sure. She said, "Take a deep breath." I'm still hesitant but try a little. "No, no," she says, "a deep breath." So here goes; I do it. "Do it again," she says, and I do it again. "Any pain?" "Nope." "Are you sure?" she asks. No pain. Okay. She calls Ronnie, her bodyguard, to come over, a blond-haired man. Ms. Kuhlman says, "Ronnie, I want you to run around this sanctuary, and Steve, you try to catch him." Off goes Ronnie, and I run after trying to catch him. After forty-five seconds, she calls me back up front. "How are we doing?" she asks. I feel good, yes, very good. Any pain? No. "Take another deep breath." Next, this medical doctor opens my shirt and places the stethoscope on my chest. "Breathe again, again, and one more time. Again." He says no infection—go, and give God all the glory. Lungs are clear. After eighty-seven days, I'm totally healed by God's grace. And all that time, I kept saying that Kathryn's not for real. She's a hoax. Yet, God loved me so much that He still healed me with all my doubts. Ms. Kuhlman always says she's not the Healer, God is—and all I could say was *"Thank You, Jesus!"*

After I signed the Healing Register book, I found myself not wanting to leave the sanctuary. Every time I would open the door to go outside, I felt the world was too dirty. Finally, a man of God approached me and said, "My son, that's where God wants you to go. Out there with His Gospel." Finally, I left. Jeremiah 30:17 *"I will restore health unto you and heal you of your wound."*

CHAPTER TWO

Thou Shalt Not Steal

When I was growing up, I had some great moments. I was about eleven years old and had a paper route. I also did errands for an Italian lady, Emma Veraldi. One day, Emma sent me to the Streamline Market for a few items. It was only a few blocks away, across the Ohio River Boulevard. Hastily, she said, "I'm giving you a check as your reward of 75 cents." It was a dividend check from her insurance company. "This is for your pocket." She'd already called the manager and asked, "Will it be alright? Young Steve will be over shortly to pick a few items." "Yes," replied the manager, "one of our cashiers can handle that."

Emma gave me the necessary money for the groceries and the check and I left. Off to the market I ran. I picked up her items and went to the checkout counter. Most of the cashiers knew me and knew that Emma had sent me, so I paid for the items and then handed her the check from the insurance company for 75 cents. Apparently, the manager had just told her that I would be in shortly and it would be okay to cash my check.

So here the lady is removing dollar bills from her register. I knew she was making a mistake but didn't say anything. After all was said and done, she gave me $19.42. My mind was already seeing a new baseball glove and baseball; a football and bat. What else? I kept my mouth shut and went back to Emma's house with her groceries. She asked if I'd cashed the check. "Yes," I answered and left.

Wow! $19.42 was a lot of money in those days. I was as nervous as a cat on a hot tin roof! How could I conceal that amount of money from my mom who knew every time I did something wrong? I went down into the cellar and wrapped the money in newspaper and placed it in the rafters. That night I dreamed a mouse was chewing on my fortune. When I awoke, I ran down to the cellar to make sure it was okay. Wow! Nothing had bothered it, so I went back to sleep. Upon awakening, I left for school, but the money was on my mind all day long. My peace was taken from me and, for some reason, I couldn't go to Honus Wagner's Sporting Store to buy my heart's desire. By the third day, I was devastated so I marched back over to the Streamline Market with the money and talked to the manager. I told him what I did, but he apparently knew nothing about the overpayment. What happened was, the cashier looked at the date [1942] and gave me that sum.

It sure was a lesson that I needed to learn because today, at 75 years of age, I haven't stolen anything since that I know of.

Exodus 20:15 (NKJV) states, *"You shall not steal,"* written in the Ten Commandments by our God.

CHAPTER THREE

The Peace That Passes All Understanding

Another time: it was Christmas Eve, 1946—a great time to be a newspaper carrier. I just finished my paper route of 52 customers and was heading home on a cold, snowy day. My customers were generous to a lad of fifteen, and I had a pocket full of monetary gifts and some goodies, ready to share with my family. On the way home, on the busy corner of Superior and California Avenues on the north side of Pittsburgh, PA, my buddy Jackie sold papers to the passing motorists.

Since it was halfway home, I stopped. Jackie always had a 55-gallon drum filled with a hot, burning fire to give all tremendous hand and body warmth. Across the intersection was St. Gabriel's Roman Catholic Church. A service was about to begin when suddenly the local shuttle bus, bringing many elderly women to church, stopped at the corner. As the women were exiting the bus, one woman was clutching her purse and a folded bag. Unbeknownst to her, she dropped her purse while still clutching the bag. She walked across the intersection and entered the church, all while Jackie and I witnessed the scene. The bus pulled away, and Jackie immediately walked to the unnoticed purse and pitched it into a nearby sewer without any of the

Thank You, Jesus!

other women seeing him do it. I was amazed that he didn't pick it up and call to their attention that their acquaintance had dropped her purse.

After all the ladies were in church, Jackie retrieved the purse from the sewer and opening it, saw the owner's name in her wallet, along with some coins and rosaries. Also in the purse were house keys, eyeglasses, and a hankie. He looked at me and said, "You didn't see anything, right?"

Inside the wallet was $48 in bills. Jackie counted out $24 and handed it to me. He kept the other half of the money and went about the business of selling papers.

I was shocked and said, "Hey, it's Christmas Eve." Jackie just laughed and said, "Merry Christmas." Then he added, "If you want to give her the purse and your cut, you can, but don't you dare squeal on me because I'm keeping my half."

I looked at her name and street address. I knew the family's name and knew the woman had a son who most guys in the neighborhood feared. Some said he was mentally unbalanced. This was his mom—ouch! Now what was I going to do? I knew I couldn't keep the $24. I wasn't raised that way. I felt her hurt when she realized her purse and personal items were all gone on Christmas Eve. Only then did I see her come out of church looking on the snowy sidewalk and steps. Yet, we both said nothing. Jackie never spoke, only his look spoke to me, "Keep your mouth shut."

I went home under conviction. Twenty-four dollars was a lot of money back then for a fifteen-year old kid. How could I do this? I felt God watching my every move. My

The Peace That Passes All Understanding

peace was gone, and tomorrow was Christmas. Some way, somehow, I'm returning her purse and my cut of $24 - but how?

On Christmas Monday, with fear and trembling, I walked to her neighborhood and after rehearsing my statement at least fifty times, rang her doorbell. She came to the door, and before I could speak, she noticed that I was holding her purse. She asked me to come in, but knowing that her son might be at home, I wanted to tell her everything before he came into the room. I told her the entire story, but couldn't tell her Jackie's last name. I couldn't squeal on my friend.

She smiled and said, "I understand," adding, "I appreciate your honesty." Then she handed me five dollars and said, "Thanks, and have a Merry Christmas." I didn't want to take the five dollars but she insisted. I thanked her and left, feeling pretty good about myself. I felt clean.

A few days later, I saw Jackie. He'd spent his $24 on a Wilson football, baseball, and glove.

The subject was never brought up again. Our lives went on.

CHAPTER FOUR

First Love

Growing up sure had its moments. Being raised in a Christian home, I can remember my first date with Mary Anne. She had to be the prettiest girl in the whole, wide world, and I was taking her to the movies. Me! Little Stevie! She was so pretty with her blonde hair and beautiful eyes - so cool! Guys, you remember those days, don't you?

The big day arrived; it was Sunday after mass. I was going to the Hippodrome Movie Theatre in Manchester, an area of Pittsburgh. However, much to my surprise, Mary Anne's parents had a plan of their own. Their daughter and Stevie would be having a chaperone for the movies! Boy, did you ever have a setback with your first love on your first date? Golly, my dreams were shattered.

So—Mary Anne, Stevie, and Olga went to the movies together. Of course, at fifteen, we walked some six miles both ways. Mary Anne, not knowing this, wore the cutest dress, one that I really liked.

All the thoughts I'd had of our first date were far different than I could have imagined. I started to feel guilty, even when I finally held Mary Anne's warm, smooth hand

First Love

in the movies.

Once inside, it was as if the devil was smirking at me, knowing that Olga was eyeballing me the whole time. I'm thinking: I'm okay, I'm okay, and who needs Olga anyway? Now, my heart isn't going "pitter-patter." No way, with the old lady, Olga (18) keeping me in line with her looks. I survived and even treated Mary Anne and good old Olga to a treat, an Isaly Klondike!

It was an experience I still remember at the age of seventy-five. No, we didn't get married because a year later at sixteen, Silvia caught my eye, even though she didn't even know I existed.

Growing up had its ups and downs. Such is life, and Mary Anne had other plans, too. God had His own plan for both of us in the years to come. Mary Anne married a great guy and raised a beautiful family. Years later, I married Dorothy; and God gifted us with three champion children then two years later led us into ministry to serve a God Who knows what's best for all of us.

CHAPTER FIVE

My Protector

Remember the movie, "The Bodyguard"? Well, I have a bodyguard, and His name is God.

In September 1949, I was a senior at David B. Oliver High School on the north side of Pittsburgh. I didn't have a steady girlfriend and attended the senior dance with a couple who, like me, were wallflowers. Since I didn't compete in sports and wasn't even close to being a star athlete, I took up dancing—my favorite diversion. I decided that holding onto an attractive girl and dancing to a hit song was a lot better than tackling a 240-pound sweaty opponent on a football field.

The band was playing the final song of the night when Renee, one of my classmates, approached me. She asked if I would escort her home. Her steady boyfriend had stood her up because of a baseball game. He was a pitcher, and I guess he considered baseball more interesting than Renee. It was around 10 p.m., and she lived three miles away. The journey to her home was through some pretty rough turf where street gangs were prevalent and at war with each other. Since her boyfriend was a first lieutenant in the turf wars, she was afraid of being caught by the opposition.

I felt I was on neutral ground. I didn't belong to a gang and had never had any problems in the neighborhood, so I offered to be her escort. The night was pleasantly warm and being with a beauty like Renee could make any guy turn his head.

We talked about high school, marriage, kids, and our plans after graduation. While Renee focused on getting married and having a nice home, I wanted to further my education, join a good company, and buy a car - not realizing Uncle Sam had other plans that involved a divided nation called Korea.

As we neared her home, we had to walk past a delicatessen. Eight members of a gang called The Manchester Boys were hanging around outside the deli. Their job was to protect their turf from any "outsiders." They watched us as we approached. They knew Renee and knew she was Eddie's girl—but who was this strange guy with her? Renee gave them a casual nod, and I waved; we continued walking. We got to the block where she lived. She thanked me, and we said good night.

I realized I had another five miles to go, so I picked up the pace heading home. That meant passing by the Manchester gang for the second time. I didn't know any of them. As I approached, they began forming a circle around me and asked what I was doing with Eddie's girl. I tried to explain, but it was like they weren't interested in what I was saying. They saw me as an intruder on their "turf," and I was their enemy.

They kept me from passing and began discussing what they should do to me. My heart was beating like a triphammer. I didn't know what to expect but could recall some stories about guys who had been found severely beaten in this part of town. I knew I could handle one of the guys—but eight? I was hopelessly outnumbered and in big trouble!

Things got awfully quiet, and I was already feeling the first blow and the pain. Suddenly, a voice spoke out loud and clear: "Don't touch him!"

I turned and recognized a big guy coming toward us from across the street. Bob and I were high school friends, and he began telling them I was okay. He also happened to be the ringleader of the Manchester turf.

Bob told them in the loud voice of a commander that I was not to be touched. While I was not a Christian in those days, I recognize today that God was in charge, telling Satan: "Don't touch him. He belongs to me."

CHAPTER SIX

His Eye Is On The Sparrow, And I Know He Watches Me

I can remember, also, a rainy Thursday during summer vacation—a good feeling having high school closed for a few months. I bid my mother goodbye and headed out the kitchen door to meet my local buddies. We always seemed to hang out on the corner of Superior Avenue and Hotchkiss Street on the north side of Pittsburgh, Pennsylvania.

It was drizzling; as usual, my buddies were all there sitting in Steve K.'s four-door 1939 Ford sedan. Inside sat Timmy, Buddy and Bones.

"What's up?" I asked. "Nothing much," Steve replied. "Any plans for the day?" "Naw," replied Steve. "Hop in and let's go for a ride."

I squeezed in the middle of the back seat. Steve put the car in gear, and we headed up Superior Avenue. "Anybody have any ideas what to do?" "Nope, not me." The other four just shrugged their shoulders. I really didn't feel like going for a ride so I said, "Drop me off at the Paramount Theater. I'll catch the matinee show. Anybody game?" No answers. So, for the next ten blocks, we just "shot the breeze."

Thank You, Jesus!

Stopping in front of the theater, I jumped out—feeling somewhat relieved after being crushed between Timmy and Bones. "See you guys later." Steve honked the horn and drove off. The rain came down heavier as I scooted up to the teller's booth for my ticket.

Almost three hours later, I left the Paramount and started my two and one-half mile walk home. Walking past the local bakery on Brighton Road, the aroma drew me inside to buy their daily special: a "Washington Pie." A favorite of mine, it was a small pie filled with the fruit of the day and placed inside an icy-covered vanilla-flavored topping. Feeling like I was starving, it didn't take long to gulp it down. I hurried my pace and headed home - wondering where Steve and the gang were and what they were doing. As I was nearing our neighborhood, it started to rain. I again broke into a run trying to get inside the kitchen door before getting soaked.

It wasn't until about 6 p.m. when someone called me at home. I picked up the phone and heard a rather shaky, nervous voice. "Hey, Totin!" "Yes," I answered, "Who is this?" The voice on the other end asked, "Did you hear about Steve K.?" "No, what happened?" The voice on the other end said, "He was in a bad car wreck." "What? Where? What happened?" "They hit a tree on Davis Avenue coming out of Riverview Park. It was raining hard, and they slid into a large oak tree head-on. Looks real bad, Totin. They were all taken to the hospital. The car was totaled. Timmy was cut severely from his shoulder to his anklebone with other lacerations. Buddy has a broken jaw and lacerations. Bobbie (Bones) died, and Steve's face was cut. The impact was so forceful that their shoes flew off."

His Eye is on the Sparrow and I Know He Watches Me

I was stunned! I was told that it happened about an hour after they dropped me off.

Why was I spared? Why did I want to go to a movie? That just wasn't my style—movies in the afternoon? God's ways are higher than my ways—only He has the answer.

After that day, I lost track of Timmy and Buddy. I did visit Steve K., who passed away months ago. He was my good friend. It was just one more time to say, *"Thank You, Jesus!"*

CHAPTER SEVEN

Lean Not To Your Own Understanding

In 1952, I [along with many young men] was drafted into the Armed Forces. After sixteen weeks of Basic Training, my orders were cut and I was assigned to the Chemical Corp. in Korea. I was standing at a railroad station in Yung Dung PO, Korea, awaiting a train to take me to Seoul, Korea. It was raining - a dark, overcast, late afternoon, and somewhat chilly. My thoughts went back home to Pittsburgh, and I wondered what mom and dad were doing just then.

Somewhat scared and not knowing my future as I faced an eighteen-month tour of duty, I wondered why at twenty-one years of age, my life had been interrupted to serve my country in a place I knew nothing about - not even their culture. There were thoughts of facing an enemy from North Korea, too.

As I looked around, I noticed a few Korean civilians with boxes tied with crude strands of rope waiting there also. To my left stood a lonely soldier, his fatigue cap somewhat cocked on his head, smoking a cigarette. To this "greenhorn" from Pennsylvania, he looked like a soldier I'd seen in many war movies: tough, rugged, unshaven. "Maybe I should hang out with him and learn the ropes so

Lean Not to Your Own Understanding

I can make it," I thought.

As I was pondering this, I noticed two M.P.'s [Military Police] walking toward this man; only then did I notice the chains and handcuffs and realize he was their prisoner - a P.O.W.

I thought, "Boy, kid, you sure can pick 'em." Smiling, I said a short prayer, "Lord, I better keep my eyes on You if I'm going to make it over here and back home to Pittsburgh in one piece."

Eighteen months later, God honored my prayers, and I arrived in the States. Feeling somewhat weak and ill, I checked in at the Veteran's Outpatient Clinic in Pittsburgh, Pennsylvania. I was told my liver was infected and sent to the Aspinwall Veteran's Hospital. Three months later, I was finally discharged. My liver survived the Hepatitis B infection as well as the jaundice I'd contracted somewhere between Seoul, Korea, and the good old United States.

On this particular day, I had a checkup at the Federal Building where the Veteran's Outpatient Clinic was located in downtown Pittsburgh. I picked up my car at the parking garage and drove over the Ninth Street Bridge. I was heading for the north side when suddenly, about twenty-five feet in front of me, a young man was running across the street with an elderly woman chasing after him. He was clutching a brown paper bag. The woman stopped running. I put my window down and asked her what was wrong. Out of breath, she could barely speak. "He just robbed my restaurant," she said. I told her to call the police and immediately started to slowly track this guy as he continued running.

Thank You, Jesus!

About four blocks later, he ran into the open parking lot of the Sears & Roebuck store. I followed him trying to stay out of his view when, out of the corner of my eye, I saw him duck behind a parked car. For the love of me, I don't know why I was in pursuit. Suddenly, he bolted out into the open space. I cut the wheels and drove straight toward him. Confused, he tried to go back to a parked car, but I was right on him. He froze as I slowly approached. His back was against the wall, and I gently pinned him up against it. Now he's looking over my hood through the windshield, and I thought, "Now what?" Thank God, he didn't have a gun. He was still clutching the brown paper bag. We just stared at each other - frozen. For how long, I don't know.

Suddenly, I realized a Pittsburgh police car was parked behind me. I watched as the police approached him. They motioned me to back up slightly, which I did. Then they cuffed him and walked him back to their patrol car, putting him in the back seat. One of the officers walked over to my car and asked, "Sir, what is your name?" I realized then that I could barely speak. Only then did I realize what fear truly is.

What made me do what I did on the spur of the moment? I'm not a police officer or hero. Only then could I understand what a person feels when they run into a burning building to rescue someone still trapped inside.

I finally told the officer that I'd rather stay out of their report. No name. No nothing. The officer asked if I was okay. "Yes, I think so." They thanked me and drove off.

I sat there for quite some time, feeling so different inside. Finally, I drove home visualizing what the police must feel every time they are called to a robbery.

CHAPTER EIGHT

Angel Unaware

I had been a member of the Pennsylvania National Guard since my Army discharge. It was Good Friday—a beautiful, sunny day. I had the day off from my workplace and decided to serve my half-day at the National Guard facility in Washington, PA—an outfit I attended one weekend each month—the 104th Air Calvary (helicopters). It was one of those days when one feels so grateful to be a Christian and live in a free society. I put in my five hours and was heading home on Interstate 79 North with a cassette tape playing worship music.

I usually don't pick up hitchhikers but noticed up ahead a man walking. I slowed the car down, pulled off the highway, rolled the window down and asked the elderly, white-haired man, "Where are you heading?" "New York City," he replied. "I'm only going to the Carnegie Exit two miles away, but if it helps, hop in." He was carrying a small handbag. I asked, "How long are you going to stay up there?" "I don't really know," he replied. "My son lives there. My wife has passed away, and there really isn't anything or anyone to hold me in West Virginia. So I'm going to stay with my son for a season."

We drove on until I was near my exit when I decided

to drive him a few more miles to where 79 North and 376 intersect, which would give him a better chance of getting a ride up 79 North to New York City. I felt I needed to do more, but I only had $3.90 on me. I offered to take him home and feed him, but he said, "No, I need all the daylight I can get"—so I gave him the $3.90 and doubled back.

I told my Dorothy, sensing he was more than a hitchhiker. She asked, "Why didn't you bring him home so I could feed him?" I told her I did offer, but he refused. She gave me twelve dollars, all she had on hand; I got back in the car and hurried back to the place I had dropped him off. As I slowed down, he came over to the car thinking I was offering him a ride. Then he realized I was the man who gave him the $3.90 earlier. I said, "Here, take this, too." He was so overwhelmed, and I repeated, "Go ahead and take it." Reluctantly, he did, and I asked the Lord to bless him. Just as I was pulling out another car came and picked him up.

I sensed in my spirit that he could have been put in my path for this purpose.

"Lord," I asked, "was he an angel?" I didn't get an answer, but it sure felt good being able to help someone during Easter week!

CHAPTER NINE

My Dorothy

On a warm, Sunday evening in 1957, while attending a dance at a Slovenian Social Club, I first saw Dorothy Bobish—an attractive blonde who would become my wife. She was in the company of two other young ladies.

This was my first visit to the club. A popular polka band that called themselves the *Glen Lads* were playing. It was common knowledge that Dorothy, along with a dozen other young people, followed the *Lads* from dance to dance like one happy family. If you loved to polka and waltz, like most Western Pennsylvanians do, this was the crowd you needed to be with.

After surveying the people present, I knew I had to approach her and ask for a dance. There was a lot of competition for her company. I watched her dance gracefully on the floor and felt her passion for dancing. My problem was I only knew the two-step. After gathering up all my courage, I walked to her table for an all-out assault. The worst she could say was "No."

She looked up at me, smiling, and I blurted out my request. I said something like, "Excuse me, but would you like to dance?" And her reply was, "Sure."

My Dorothy

I thought I'd better be honest and quickly explained my lack of experience with the polka. "No problem," she responded. If I could only do the two-step, she would settle for number eight - to explain, my dancing talent was only the slow two-step. "Okay," she said, "number eight." Dorothy patiently explained that number one represented the polka, number two was a waltz, three was the jitterbug, and number four was the slow dance. I was eighth in line and would have to wait for my dance.

When the dance finally came around, I held her very gently and respectfully. I was very nervous! Normally not one at a loss for words, tonight I wanted to be a perfect gentleman because this girl really impressed me.

As my nerves settled down, I asked if she came to the dance every Sunday. "No," she replied. "Not every Sunday, but I come quite often." Nervously, I repeated, "Do you come here every Sunday?" She replied, "No." The small talk was getting me nowhere. She was nearly as uptight as I felt, but she danced like a professional. I prayed I wouldn't step on her dainty foot with my size elevens.

When the dance ended, I thanked her and accompanied her back to her table. With apprehension, I asked if she had any other dances left on her ticket. She jokingly responded, "A slow one?" I nodded, and she said, "How about number 12?" I said that would be fine, and we shook hands.

Meeting Dorothy on that memorable Sunday evening was the beginning of a changed life for me. At the time, I didn't realize it was ordained by God. I really wasn't that much interested in church in those days. On the way home with my two friends, Ted and Joe, I was unusually quiet.

Thank You, Jesus!

My thoughts had been captivated by a blonde beauty with the most incredible green eyes. All I knew was I had enjoyed a great time and wanted to repeat it.

My pals dropped me off first but not before I found out where the regular dance crowd hung out every Wednesday. The place was the Bel-Aire in Bridgeville. I began showing up each Wednesday night at the club and began building a friendship with the blonde from Cherry Valley, Pennsylvania.

There was something special about Dorothy that kept me coming back for more of her company. I found myself wanting to be wherever she was. I had a lot of competition, since dancing was her total enjoyment. The guys that showed up at these dance spots were good friends of Dorothy's and the other girls. They were like big brothers, protecting them from outsiders like me.

Dorothy always arrived alone in her Ford. That meant taking her home was out of the question. After a month, I decided to be bold. "Can I follow you home?" I blurted out. She wanted to know why, and I responded, "To get to know you better." She hesitated for a moment and said, "I don't think that's such a good idea." That pretty much terminated the talk - conversation ended. When the dance ended, she drove off by herself; and I went back home to the north side of Pittsburgh.

For the next few weeks, I had to work 3-12 p.m. and couldn't visit the Bridgeville dance, even though I wanted to see her again. I found myself hoping she was thinking of me just as much as I was thinking of her. About a month passed before I saw Dorothy again. I discovered she wasn't

My Dorothy

there either on those same weeks that I missed. Jealousy was starting to take me over, but I didn't have the courage to tell her. I was fearful of rejection. She might even have put me down with: "Who do you think you are? I'm not your girl, and I can dance with anyone I want." So I kept my thoughts to myself.

The next time I saw her, I summoned all the courage I could and asked her for a date the following Saturday. She stunned me by saying she was free and, yes, she would go out with me. I felt like I was walking two feet off the ground when she gave me directions to her home in Cherry Valley.

It was quite a distance from Pittsburgh's north side to the Bobish farm, but I didn't mind it a bit. She introduced me to her mother, Mary. Her mother was very pleasant and managed to put me at ease. We talked some, and I assured her mother that I would take good care of Dorothy—I wouldn't keep her out too late, even though her daughter was 22, and I was 26. That respect seemed to earn me some good points with Mrs. Bobish.

We left the house and drove to downtown Pittsburgh where I had picked out a club that had a combo and dance floor. It felt almost like Heaven, and the evening turned out to be a perfect start to a lifelong relationship. We dated more often and started going steady. There was no doubt in my heart, and she felt the same. She met my folks, and she and my mom hit it off. In 1958, I gave her an engagement ring. I was ready to be a husband and a father - I was 27, Dorothy was 23.

CHAPTER TEN

Goodbye, City Life!

The young lady I was planning to marry lived on a farm - a haven of peace and quiet, away from the hustle and bustle of city life. Until I met Dorothy, I hadn't spent much time on a farm, being a city boy.

After our wedding on October 10, 1959, most Sundays after church, Dorothy and I would be invited to her parents' home for dinner. Her mother, Mary, was an excellent cook. Knowing I loved veal cutlets, Mom Bobish made sure they were breaded; and she always made sure my plate was full of roast beef, mashed potatoes, and corn. She always included dessert, so one could see why Dorothy was also an excellent cook.

After dinner, while Dorothy and her mother shared some time, I loved to walk up through the pasture to the peak of the farm-hoping I wouldn't run into any of Dad Bobish's cattle. Those Holstein cows and ol' Steve just never got along - what with me being a "city slicker" as Dad called me.

One day, Dad Bobish told his son, Eddie, to take an eighteen-month old heifer over to the next farm belonging to Mr. Kaski to have his bull mate it, adding, "Take Steve

Goodbye, City Life!

with you."

I knew I was in trouble now and had no idea what was going to happen in the next hour. I don't know if Dad knew I was afraid of cows and horses, so off Eddie and I went - leading the heifer to some lovemaking with Mr. Bull.

About a hundred yards away, I heard a scary, weird, sound. I asked, "What's that?" Eddie replied, "The bull knows this heifer is in heat." Being a city slicker, even I knew that. "Where's he at?" "In the barn," replied Eddie.

The sun had gone down, and night was fast approaching. Finally, we reached the barn. Mr. Kaski had received a phone call that Eddie and Steve were coming, so he came out of the barn and invited us in. I thought - there's always a first time!

I'd never been to a heifer and bull date, so Eddie placed two ropes on the heifer: one on the right side of the bridle, and one attached to the left-side bridle. We each took a rope and started to back the animal into a narrow, long-looking stall. Mr. Kaski disappeared for the moment.

Both Eddie and I were on the outside of this stall when Eddie said, "Steve, hold onto the rope tightly. Don't let it go, so this heifer can't move." Just then I heard a squeaky door open behind me, and out came an ugly black bull - his eyes like fire with the barn lights shining into them. Then Mr. Kaski started to poke at the bull with a long-handled pitchfork to get him to move. I couldn't believe that this big bull was going to jump on the little heifer. Eddie warned me again, "Don't let off the rope!" Suddenly, this bull takes off and leaps on top of the heifer. I shut my eyes and felt a heavy tug on the rope. When I opened my

Thank You, Jesus!

eyes, the heifer was down on her knees, and Mr. Kaski was driving the bull back up the stall. He yelled, "Okay, Eddie, let's try again."

The bull made a second pass, but this time leaped on the left side of the heifer; the bull's head missed *my* head by inches as the heifer started to fall again. At that moment - you guessed it! - I let the rope go. Eddie yelled, "Steve! Pick up the rope!" It was inside the stall, and Mr. Bull was looking right at me as I tried to reach inside. Mr. Kaski hit the bull on the neck trying to force him back up the stall. By now, Mr. Kaski said, "Eddie, it's no use. Take her back to your dad's. Tell him to butcher her."

We started back to Dad's farm. Golly, I thought, it's all my fault. This heifer is going to die because of me. I became very quiet.

I asked Eddie not to mention to his Dad that I let the rope go. Eddie said, "Don't worry, I won't mention you." I never knew if Mr. Kaski said anything. Two days later, the death warrant was issued and the heifer was gone.

I didn't eat veal or beef for a few weeks. Dorothy knew I felt horrible about this poor animal, but she assured me that's farm life. Years later, Dad quit raising livestock, and I had peace.

CHAPTER ELEVEN

Don't Be Deceived

In 1958, I became employed by the G.F. Otto Ice Cream Manufacturing Company on the north side of Pittsburgh. We produced ice cream for the Kroger and A&P grocery story chains.

I was placed in the Loading Truck Department, starting at 3:30 until whatever time it took to load fifteen route trucks and one tractor trailer. After one month, I joined the Local 205 Teamster Union of Dairymen & Chauffeurs of American and was accepted. Being young and basically in good physical shape, lifting racks of ice cream and working in subzero temperature in their freezer warehouse paid a good wage and provided benefits. After four years, a new job opened in the Sterilization Department, and my bid was accepted.

Months later, I was approached by the General Manager and offered the position of Night Turn Supervisor. I was told that I could still be a teamster and company man, too. I accepted and enjoyed a great relationship with both sides. I was chosen because I was honest, I was told. The devil was about to test me.

One day, a local Fire Chief drove onto the property in

Thank You, Jesus!

his red Fire Chief's car and said that he'd come for his ice cream order. I asked for the purchasing order receipt, and he said, "Oh, I have no need of one since I have a contract with your company." I was the only supervisor on the loading dock at the time and felt it was okay to release his order to him. Hey, he was the Fire Chief. What wrong would he do? I even put the order together for him and placed it in his car. He thanked me and drove off after scribbling his name on my itemized order form. I turned in his receipt and went on with my work order for the day.

The next day, after checking in, I was called to the front office by Mr. Ed Marxen, the General Manager and my boss. He said, "Steve, how often do you give out ice cream without a paid receipt?" I said, "Oh, never. It's not company policy." He smiled some and asked, "Then why did you give the local Fire Chief an order of ice cream?" "Oh," I said, "He has a contract with our corporation, sir." "No, he doesn't," Mr. Marxen said. "No one ever gets free ice cream again. "Is that understood? You need a paid receipt." "Yes, sir, I understand."

I had been had big time and even put it in his car for him. Of course, you know what happened when my crew heard what a dumb thing I fell for—a lot of ribbing. From that day on, I walked squeaky clean; no paid sales receipt—no ice cream. I repented—big time. Until the summer months ... when a white Chevy Impala pulled onto the loading dock and a very well-dressed lady called to me and said, "Son, please fill this order" and handed me a note of about eight items. "You're new here." "Yes," I said. She laughed and said, "I'm Mrs. Otto, Tom's wife, owner of this company." I replied, "Sure you are, and I'm the Pope!"

Don't Be Deceived

With that remark, she got a little uptight, got out of her car and went into the dairy. I thought, "Okay, sweetheart. I ain't falling for that a second time." Maybe I'm being tested for loyalty, I thought.

A few minutes later, my name was called over the intercom system. "Steve Totin, report to the front office, pronto." So, up the stairs I hustle; and there in Mr. Marxen's office stood this pretty lady and a red-faced Ed Marxen, the General Manager. "Steve," he said kind of funny, "This is Tom Otto's wife. How could you have talked to her in that tone of voice?" All the time he's chewing me out, she's smiling and nodding her head in agreement.

I said, "Sir, when I am in charge, no one gets any products from me without a paid purchase order form—no one!" Mr. Marxen's jaw dropped, and Mrs. Otto burst out laughing and said, "Ed, we need more employees like Steve. He's going to do alright here."

So, I personally met Mrs. Tom Otto that day. Curious, Ed Marxen asked, "What made you doubt she was who she said she was?" "Because why would she be driving a Chevy when Mr. Otto drives a Caddy? That's why I questioned her. She could be anybody." I stayed with the dairy for fifteen years as their foreman until it went out of business.

CHAPTER TWELVE

Fear Creates Havoc

During our years of marriage, I underwent five major surgeries—causing us to fall into debt. Doing what most people do, I borrowed money from a lending institution. Paying back a loan at 18.5% interest and raising a family can truly cause you more pain than having surgery.

After falling behind on a monthly payment, I received some very nasty letters from the lending corporation manager - pay up or else! We were doing the best we could, but I did miss a month here and there.

I talked with a lawyer, and he suggested that I not try to avoid them but pay back fifty cents on the dollar, which I did. But the home office wasn't satisfied and started to call again and threaten me all the more.

One day, between being in physical pain and talking to this gentleman, I reached my peak of despair. He said, "Listen to me. If I don't get a full payment in twenty-four hours, I'm going to fix your wagon." I wondered what in the world that meant. Am I being threatened? My God, is he going to send someone to physically hurt me or my wife or three children? So - I decided to hurt him first.

Fear Creates Havoc

The next day, he called and again asked, "Did you send the payment I requested?" I replied, "No can do - only a partial payment." Gosh, was he upset! After being called a wise guy, I'd had it and said, "Listen very carefully, sir, to what I'm about to say." With that, I opened the kitchen door and threw the phone handset as hard as I could. It hit the concrete and shattered the phone - with me hoping his ear would never be the same again. Thank God, Dorothy wasn't home - she would have really chewed me out! Next, I called the phone company for repairs, indicating the receiver had slipped out of my hand. Of course, when the repairman arrived, he didn't say much. I believe he knew the truth.

About a week later, and I'd had no more threatening calls from the lending manager. I was at work during the 3-11 p.m. shift when I decided to call Dorothy as I usually did, just to say "Hi." The phone rang, and she answered, "Hello." I said, "Hon, it's me." Again, she said, "Hello, is anyone there?" Again, I answered, "Hon, it's me." I could hear her, but she couldn't hear me. I hung up and dialed again. The same thing happened. She couldn't hear me. So I thought - now what? No cell phones back in the '60s - and I allowed fear to take over. I thought she was being "entertained" by someone from the lending agency office against her will and could only respond by saying "Hello."

I left my place of employment and drove home, parked in the street behind our home, and climbed over the fence. Creeping up to our kitchen window, I peeked in and saw Dorothy in the kitchen talking to our three small children. Everything looked okay. I tapped on the window, and she pushed the curtain aside as she said, "Why are you out there and not at work?" It was 8 p.m. I came around to the

Thank You, Jesus!

door and went in. "What are you doing home so early?" she asked. "Honey, I tried to call you, but you couldn't hear me." "Oh," she said, "I had four or five calls like that with no one on the other end." Dorothy knew nothing about the threatening phone call from the lending manager.

After I was assured that she and the children were safe, I returned to work. That month, I saw to it that a full payment was made. But three weeks later, Dorothy called and said, "Steve, can you come home right now?" Dorothy was never fearful, but the tone of her voice said, "Come quickly!" I asked what was wrong. Again, she said, "Please come now!" I left hurriedly. When I arrived home, she told me to call the Scott Township police. I called and a sergeant said, "Sir, we took a call from a neighbor on your street who said she was troubled by a man ringing her doorbell and anxiously knocking on her door. He kept calling the name 'Steve - Steve, open up!' This poor woman was home by herself with five little children, so she called out her second floor window saying, 'There is no Steve here.' That's when she noticed a gun in his waistband.

"Quickly, she closed the window and called us. When we arrived, we couldn't find him so, Steve, we suggest you keep your lights off and don't walk by your windows." Then the sergeant asked, "Do you know anyone who wants to hurt you?" I thought of the manager's threat: "I'm gonna fix your wagon." Oh my God - he really wasn't kidding! So, I told the sergeant everything. "Okay, Steve," he said, "Don't use or answer your phone. We have an unmarked police car watching your home, and we'll contact you with a signal of three rings, a pause, and two more rings." Okay … I thought for sure there was a contract on me for not paying the loan. Finally, I told Dorothy the whole story.

Fear Creates Havoc

Now I had the serious thought—my lovely family is in danger because of me!

Were you ever so fearful that you imagine noises and shadows in your home? I did. Those hours we waited, wondering who this man was—we couldn't do anything but pray. Fear can paralyze you, and we felt so helpless.

Finally, hours later, the phone rang. Three times… two times. I answered it. It was the sergeant. "Steve?" "Yes," I said. "We have him. Can you come to the station?" It was almost one a.m., and a police car was still in front of our home. They stayed, and I drove our car to the police station. Entering the jail, I was still upset. Did I have to face this man? Who was he?

When I saw the man, I realized I knew him. It was Pat - someone I'd talked with numerous times. Pat said, "Steve, I looked and looked for you and didn't know which house you lived in. I needed to talk to you."

You see, Pat was grieving. His only close friend was his dad who had died; a father who gave his son an old gun, minus a firing pin. Pat treasured this gift from his dad and took it everywhere he went. Pat was a disabled vet, and he would unload all his hurts and pain as I talked and prayed with him - I would just be there in his time of need.

Yes, fear does create havoc.

CHAPTER THIRTEEN

God Knows My Thoughts

Deloris Weiss was a close friend of my Dorothy and me. For years, she lived in Scott Township, as we did, a suburb of Pittsburgh, Pennsylvania.

Deloris was a sincere Christian who was married to a Jewish businessman. They were blessed with two children, Matthew and Julie.

The time came for Matt to make his Bar Mitzvah, and we were invited to the ceremony. Dorothy decided that only I should attend, and now I'm sitting in their temple as a first-timer.

Not knowing what to expect, I received a yarmulke at the door, took my seat about halfway down, and placed the skullcap on my head hoping it wouldn't slip off. I was amazed that all the men sat in the sanctuary with a screen separating them from the women. A man sat down beside me, and we exchanged greetings. Later, I found out he was a dentist by profession. The man on my right was also a medical doctor.

Before the service began, the dentist started talking to me, asking if I was a relative of Matthew. I answered,

God Knows My Thoughts

"Good friend." Then I explained that this was my first time in a temple. He asked me about my profession, and I told him that I was in ministry - an evangelist for Jesus Christ. "Sounds interesting," he said. "Very much so," I replied. He asked, "Where do you evangelize?" I said, "Well, I'm with Cornerstone TeleVision, a Christian TV station. I have a prison ministry, and I tell inmates about a better life for now and eternity." A few moments later, the service started. It was quite interesting hearing the chants and the reading of the Torah.

As we were departing, the dentist asked if I planned to attend the banquet that evening. "Yes," I answered. He replied, "Steve, you're an interesting person to talk to. I enjoyed our talk."

At 7 p.m. that evening, my wife Dorothy and I walked into a ballroom located in the Oakland section of Pittsburgh. We found our assigned table with six others and exchanged greetings. Matthew's father approached me and said, "Steve, my mother asked me to say this. She would love to have a dance with you sometime tonight." I smiled and tried to discourage him, telling him that I was not a good dancer. In my thoughts, I was thinking, "I don't want to dance with anyone except my lovely Dorothy." Dorothy smiled and said, "You'll be okay. Just relax."

Dinner was served. Finally the ceremony began, and it was very nice. I enjoyed the ritual. As it ended, the dentist I met in the temple approached me and said, "Steve, would you please come and meet my wife?" So Dorothy and I walked over to their table and exchanged greetings. The dentist's wife smiled and said, "My husband could not say enough about the man he met in the temple." We thanked

Thank You, Jesus!

them and went back to our table.

The music began, and the dance floor started to fill with couples. Dorothy and I joined in and danced a few numbers then sat down. Dorothy knew I was uptight, fearing Mr. Weiss' mother was coming soon. All along God knew. I kept saying, "Please, Lord, spare me this dance. I would rather not." Ever so often, I could see her at the bar. Even in her late 70's, she sounded like a livewire.

Then it happened - Mr. Weiss came to me and said, "Steve, mom changed her mind." *"Thank You, Jesus!"* Whew! I smiled and jokingly said, "Well, that's the first time a million dollars slipped out of my hands." His mom was a millionaire twice.

Be My Witness

Deloris' father, after being ill for a long spell, closed his eyes and passed away. Deloris called and asked if I would come to his viewing in Penn Hills, Pennsylvania, and share a few words on her dad's behalf. I arrived at the funeral home on the day of his burial and shared, along with the local pastor.

I wasn't planning to go to the cemetery, but Deloris said, "Steve, please come, too." The funeral director said I could ride with the pallbearers in a stretch limo. Upon entering the vehicle, I realized I did not know the other five men. All the bearers were friends and businessmen. A few moments passed, and I introduced myself to the others and they did likewise. Then the question was asked of me: how did I know the Weiss family? I explained that I met Deloris first since she attended the prayer meeting held at our home each Friday. Through her, I met her husband Julius

God Knows My Thoughts

and their children. We were also praying for her father and his sickness. One man asked, "Are you a minister?" I replied, "Yes." Another man's expression was a slight smile. The rest did not say or do anything, and it got awfully quiet. Then one man asked, "Where do you minister? Do you have a church?" I replied, "No church building, but I am employed at Cornerstone TeleVision in Wall, Pennsylvania. It's a Christian TV station, and I minister to whoever calls for prayer." I told them about Jesus dying on Calvary, so each man heard about salvation.

We were now entering the cemetery and proceeded to the chapel. On the ride back to the funeral parlor to pick up our cars, one of the men drove back in another car and a new man got into our limo. Everyone knew him except me. I said, "I'm Steve." He replied, "Mike." One other man remarked to this new rider, "Don't ask Steve what he does." I chuckled to myself and could see Jesus smiling, as if to say, "Light and darkness don't mix too well, Steve." I quietly said, "Amen."

CHAPTER FOURTEEN

Through the Fire

Years have gone by - I was laid off from the dairy. It was August 1978. A local pastor, Russ Bixler's wife, Norma, was directed by God to build a Christian television station located in Wall, Pennsylvania. Pastor Bixler hired two engineers from the PTL Club ministry in Charlotte, North Carolina.

I was introduced to Wayne Fast and Allen McCarty as a helper or "gofer" - go for this or go for that. Western Pennsylvania Christian Broadcasting, also known as WPCB, was the first Christian television station in Pennsylvania. I was told it was some 25 miles from my home. Of course, I'd never heard of Wall, Pennsylvania, and I knew absolutely nothing about television. So there I was - digging ditches, stringing cable, and attaching connectors to miles of cable - helping whoever needed a third hand, and picking up parts and supplies - day in and day out.

As news started to leak out, interested partners would drive up the mountain road in Wall to watch the erection of their Christian station.

One day, a friend of mine named Ted showed up. He had some long talks with the founder, Pastor Bixler. He

Through the Fire

even offered to take me to lunch. Several days later, Ted returned. Not being aware of his intentions, he and Russ spoke. Again, Ted offered to take me to lunch, but I refused. Time simply didn't allow for it.

Then something unusual began to happen. In our mailbox at home, a crisp fifty dollar bill was sent to me with no name of sender or return address. Money for our family was tight in those days after being laid off from the dairy after fifteen years of service. Dorothy and I and our sons, Steven and Gregory, accepted this blessing as from the Lord. The wages given to me by WPCB were a lot less. I thought whoever God was using to send us fifty dollars each week surely doesn't know how much it meant to us. I was looking at my mailbox weekly and - you guessed it! - after three weeks, the money stopped. God wanted me to trust Him; and here I was trusting my mailbox!

A dear friend, Ruthie Thompson, a godly woman of prayer, called me shortly after this and told me that she was instructed by the Holy Spirit to call and tell me to read Psalm 55:20-21 because, unbeknownst to me, a friend was about to betray me.

I continued working on the mountain and, by 1979, the work was completed. Knowing I would be out of work, Reverend Bixler asked if I would stay on and put together the phone prayer line ministry. I accepted.

On Easter Sunday, 1979, with the leading of the Holy Spirit and many partners in prayer, we went on the air for the very first time. It truly was Resurrection Sunday for WPCB, which had gone through the fire more than once, as the enemy tried desperately to stop the construction of

Thank You, Jesus!

God's television station.

I was officially hired in 1979 as a full-time employee.

One day, out of curiosity, I asked Reverend Bixler why Ted was visiting so much but never pitched in to help out as a volunteer as so many others did. Reverend Bixler said, "Ted wanted your job. He tried to convince me that he could do a better job than you and suggested I let you go." Apparently, Ted and his wife were partners [in building the television station]. Reverend Bixler said he couldn't do it because he knew "God had sent Steve to be part of the television station."

After many weeks on the air, our precious Lord provided a ministry for Ted in North Dakota for six months. I knew that Ted was a good man and loved the Lord as I did. Years later, I asked him to join my department as a Prayer Phone Captain, and he accepted.

I told Reverend Bixler that I would stay until the Lord told me differently. It's been thirty-two years, and I'm still here as His servant.

CHAPTER FIFTEEN

Prayer Changes Situations

In 1999, God gave me the vision to install an eighteen-inch satellite dish and receiver into prisons throughout America enabling inmates to view Cornerstone TeleVision. It was on December 4, 1999, that I was communicating with a women's prison in Newport, Arkansas, by letter. A door opened to install two satellite dishes: one in McPherson Unit (women's) and another in the Grimes Unit (male inmates) at the same site.

In this women's prison, a young mother was incarcerated after being charged with murdering her two small children then trying to end her own life after an abusive marriage. She survived the poisoning—the children didn't. All she wanted was to be put to death in order to be with her children. Since she was isolated from the prison population, she didn't have any television viewing privileges, which was called to my attention. After many months and many refusals from the Arkansas D.O.C. (Department of Corrections), and after much prayer, the warden said, "Okay, let's hook up her cell to view Cornerstone's programs 24/7."

So for the next eight months, she had more peace with God, viewing television, until the day of her execution.

Thank You, Jesus!

It was quitting time at my place of employment, Cornerstone TeleVision Network, in Wall, Pennsylvania. I punched out at 2:50 p.m. and headed down the long roadway toward the left turn onto Route 48 North.

As I made the turn, about six car-lengths ahead of me, a flagman was stopping traffic in both the north and southbound lanes. A construction Caterpillar was being loaded onto a flatbed tractor trailer, so we just sat there and waited. I was the first vehicle, so I motioned to the flagman and asked, "Why a Caterpillar?" He replied that a broken waterline was being repaired, and the job completed. By this time, traffic was backing up in both directions. I was waiting, facing downhill northward. Being a warm, humid day, tempers were rising as it was a slow pace loading this equipment on the flatbed. I prayed for patience waiting for the "go-ahead" sign.

Finally, the flagman motioned that our lane could go but the oncoming lane uphill was still stalled because the tractor was in their way.

I thanked God and started down the hill first, going about thirty-five miles per hour and was almost at the bottom of the roadway when an impatient female motorist decided to try to turn around and take another route. Unbeknownst to me, she finally put her vehicle in position to pull out without even looking to see if my lane was clear.

She couldn't see me, and I couldn't see her. All I saw was a long line of cars waiting.

Then it happened. Not easing out slowly, she pulled out quickly about twelve feet in front of me. I saw a portion of her car in my peripheral vision and slammed on my brakes to avoid hitting her. My Nissan Altima started to slide, pulling to the right, thank God. With a loud screeching of tires; I stopped as she continued to come out almost hitting my left front fender and door and then stopped. She truly had scared the heck out of me.

I looked at her thinking to myself, "Lady, what were you thinking?" Then I continued on, a little shell-shocked, thanking God that I was still in one piece, with another twenty-five miles to go before I was safely in my own driveway. Another *"Thank You, Jesus!"*

CHAPTER SIXTEEN

Prison Ministry

"I am not ashamed of the Gospel of Jesus Christ"

It was 1987, and my dear wife, Dorothy, and I were invited to a Christian organization, the Full Gospel Businessmen's Fellowship in New Kensington, Pennsylvania. They were having their monthly dinner, and I was asked to share my personal testimony on "forgiveness."

It was during this evening that I gave an altar call. Many came forward for prayer, including a young man named Rocco Morelli, who was awaiting sentencing to a state correctional facility in Pennsylvania. Rocco asked if I would pray for him.

This was his first time being incarcerated, so Dorothy and I both prayed for Rocco, asking God to protect him. I told him that he needed salvation, and Rocco prayed a prayer of salvation, sincerely inviting Jesus Christ into his heart and confessing he was a sinner who needed to forgive someone he held a grudge against after hearing my testimony on forgiveness.

This birthed my prison ministry, and God started to open doors for me to visit local prisons and pray with inmates. I

Prison Ministry

also went on-air at Cornerstone TeleVision in Wall, Pennsylvania, sharing and reading letters of testimony from the inmates I visited and those who called my office for prayer. I was also blessed to lead inmates to Jesus Christ as their Lord and Savior.

Allow me to share about those incarcerated. Not all those locked down are guilty of the crimes they are charged with.

Most people do not feel comfortable visiting or even talking to those confined in prisons. Even on the phone, until I was called by God to minister to those confined, I, too, shied away and felt they were all guilty. It's been twenty-two years in the prison ministry and, believe me, I've met and made friends with some great men and women who really aren't bad people but people who made bad choices in life, causing them to be confined. A lot of them have gone to prison only because they couldn't afford the right attorney to defend them.

The first time that I visited the maximum security prison in Louisiana called Angola, I, too, was uptight - knowing there were 5,300 men serving long sentences for all types of crimes and 82% will never, ever be free.

It was at Angola where I met young men who were raised in Christian homes serving long terms and even life sentences like Don, Daryl, Ron, Greg and Larry - who I've come to know and love. Yes, like so many others, they've made peace with their God, knowing He'll never leave nor forsake them.

I also remember Woody in a Colorado prison - a highly decorated Marine who served in Vietnam. He laid down

Thank You, Jesus!

his life for his country - received thirty wounds to his body, earned four Purple Hearts and two Bronze Stars given to him by presidents; yet he sits in his cell, forgotten by America year after year.

Today, our Lord has given me men and women from seventy prisons in twenty-two states, allowing me to share His love with them.

The list goes on and on. So remember - if you know someone confined … don't put them down … kneel down and say a prayer for them. It will help.

"...for I was hungry and you gave Me food; I was thirsty and you gave Me drink; I was a stranger and you took Me in; I was naked and you clothed Me; I was sick and you visited Me; I was in prison and you came to Me."

(Matthew 25:35-36 NKJV)

CHAPTER SEVENTEEN

God Honors Obedience

Telethon time to support the ministry was nearing, and I was concerned about what I was going to wear for the two weeks on-air. Having only one sport coat and no suits, I wanted to at least borrow an extra sports coat for the event.

Bill Krobot, my friend and an insurance salesman, had clothes, so I called and asked if I could borrow a sport coat for two weeks and explained why. I could live with one sport coat after the telethon.

Bill's reply was, "No - I want you to go to Gimbel's Department Store and purchase a new suit, the best they sell." After much arguing, I realized that Bill wouldn't take "No" for an answer, so I picked up his credit card and headed for the South Hills Village Mall. I entered Gimbel's Department Store and made a beeline to the Men's Department.

Much to my surprise, a huge sale on men's suits was in progress - two for $99.99. A large pile of suits were on a table, and many women were selecting two or more suits for their loved ones. I could barely get to the table to at least try and find size 46 Long. The suits were in disarray, and I never knew that women acted this way! A salesman

Thank You, Jesus!

approached me and asked if he could help. I asked him if these suits that were on sale were seconds. "Nope," he replied. "Why so cheap?" I asked, and he said that newer styles would be coming in. I finally found two suits and gave him Bill's credit card.

As I was leaving, I noticed that the salesman was crippled and walked with a bad limp. It was just then that I heard God's voice, "Steve, pray for him." "Oh, no, I'm in a hurry to get to work," but the real reason was that I was embarrassed even to approach him - so I hurried home feeling somewhat guilty, knowing my Heavenly Father was displeased.

I arrived at Bill's home and showed him my blessings. Not one suit, but two. Bill wasn't too happy with my decision and remarked, "Didn't I tell you to buy the best they had?" "But, Bill, two for one," I argued. I was happy, but Bill wasn't. Of course, I didn't tell him about my disobedience in not praying for the salesman's affliction since Bill is a praying Christian also. Much to my surprise, Bill said, "Steve, I am not paying for two sale suits. Go back and exchange these for their best." "No, I can't, or I won't," was my inner thought. Bill wasn't taking "No" for an answer, so back to Gimbel's I went. It wasn't about the suits; it was about my disobedience to my God.

The salesman saw me coming and asked if there was a problem. Sheepishly, I told him that there was. "The suit is a gift from a friend," I explained, "and he specifically said, 'Gimbel's best.'" So I exchanged the two suits and got their best for a cost of $375, which he had in other styles and colors. After paying him, I said, "Sir, I'm a Christian, and during my first visit God told me to pray for your disability and I didn't - too much pride in me. I believe this exchange is His doing. Can I pray for you?" "Yes," was his answer, "but not on the floor. Let's go into the fitting room." We did, and I prayed for God's healing upon him.

Then he added, "After you left this morning, a medical surgeon bought two suits and said, 'Sir, I can correct your hip,' and now you're here praying for me. This is awesome." "Yes," I answered, "God loves you very much, sir," and I left. Whew! I could only say, *"Thank You, Jesus!"*

CHAPTER EIGHTEEN

Fear Not, I Am With You

It was 9:15 a.m., when my office phone rang. The caller was our receptionist, Rose, who asked me to please come to the lobby.

"What's up?" I asked.

Rose shrugged, "I just sent a man to the Chapel. He wants to talk with Dave Kelton."

Dave was our General Manager. I knew he wasn't planning on coming in that day because he was working at home on a special project. I asked Rose if she had told him that. She said she had indeed given him the message, and he flatly refused to leave until he saw Dave.

"Maybe you could minister to him," she suggested. "He seems pretty troubled."

That was fine with me. I crossed the hallway, stepped into the Chapel and extended my hand. "I'm Steve Totin, Phone Ministry Director. Can I help you?"

He responded with a tense, "No, I want to see Dave. It's personal." I repeated what Rose said earlier and suggested he come back another time.

Fear Not, I am With You

I could feel pure evil in the way he stared at me. He looked like an agitated wolf on the prowl and said he had no plans to leave until he first talked with Dave. I apologized for Dave not being there and said he should have called first and saved himself an unnecessary trip. I got up to leave and that was when Dave Kelton walked through the front door.

Rose and I were both startled by his sudden appearance. I quickly spoke up and told him a man was sitting in the Chapel and wanted to talk to him. Dave asked why he was there, and I told him I had no idea - only that he seemed obsessed with discussing something with him and that he appeared to be very bothered.

"Okay, Steve. I'll see him," said Dave. "But why don't you come along with me until I see what's on his mind?" "No problem," I said. As we entered the chapel Dave introduced himself. "Hi, I'm Dave, the General Manager."

The man said his name was Jack, and that he had just finished reading Dave's book, *"Chosen to Live."* Before Dave had a chance to respond, Jack said in an angry voice that he didn't believe a word of it.

Dave took the criticism like a gentleman.

"That's fine," he said. "You're entitled to your own opinion. But what don't you believe in it?"

"Everything," Jack snapped. "It's all lies!"

Dave asked him if he was a Cornerstone partner, and Jack said he wasn't. Dave asked him if he wasn't a partner—how did he find out about the book. That was when the real story of why he was there came out.

Thank You, Jesus!

"My mother supports your ministry," he said. "She received the book as a gift for her donation." When Dave asked if he was from the area, Jack's anger seemed to increase as he answered he was from out of state. Keeping his voice calm, Dave then asked where he called home. Jack said he was from Oklahoma, unemployed, and depressed after losing his job as a roughneck in the oil fields. In addition, the bank had taken his car. All the while Jack was talking he kept his hands inside his jacket pockets.

Suddenly, he blurted, "Dave, you are a ***** liar! Nothing you wrote in that book is true!"

I was silently praying for this disturbed man who seemed on the verge of exploding. I could tell Dave was ready to end a conversation that had turned into a diatribe.

"I'm sorry you feel this way," he started to say. That was when the man pulled a revolver out of his pocket.

"You're a liar," he repeated. "I'm going to kill you."

I couldn't believe my eyes. Even worse, I was standing in front of Jack and would be the first person to receive the bullets if he started firing. Dave later told me my eyes looked like two large black olives as I stared at the .38 Special.

This was the first time in my life anyone had pointed a gun at me, and I simply froze. Dave came up with an inspiration that could only have come from the Heavenly Father.

He said quietly, in total control, "How about selling me the gun? I'll give you seventy-five dollars for it."

Fear Not, I am With You

I think Jack was as surprised to hear those words as I was.

"What did you say?" he asked.

"I told you. Would you like seventy-five dollars in exchange for your pistol?"

Time seemed to hang like eternity. Nobody moved or talked. Finally, Jack lowered the gun—and handed it over to Dave! It was a brilliant, inspired moved! I felt like shouting!

Before giving him the money, Dave opened the chamber and removed all six bullets. He thanked Jack for selling him the gun. I was still shaking inside and couldn't believe how cool he handled the situation.

Jack wanted to know what he planned to do with the .38. Dave smiled, "Keep it as a souvenir for my second book."

We took some time ministering with a suddenly very contrite Jack. He prayed with us for deliverance from a demon spirit of hatred and murder, and we all said "Amen! In Jesus' Name!"

The poor man had wounded himself for so long. He told us he left his hometown in Oklahoma and came to Pittsburgh to visit his mother. During his visit, he found a copy of Dave's book and read how God had changed Dave Kelton from an alcohol and drug abuser to becoming General Manager of a Christian TV station - Channel 40.

We prayed for Jack's salvation. Before Jack left, Dave invited him to his upstairs office for a private consultation.

Thank You, Jesus!

Later, I learned he had talked to the bank manager about getting his repossessed car back and finding him a job.

And the man had called Dave a "liar!" *Thank You, Jesus!* May Your truth rule forever!

CHAPTER NINETEEN

No Weapon Formed Against Me Shall Prosper

It's Friday, May 11, 2007. It's been eighteen months to the day that my lovely Dorothy went to heaven. It was a day of mixed emotions. Being alone now and with the two-day weekend ahead, I left Cornerstone TeleVision, my place of employment, and started my twenty-five mile journey home to Scott Township, Pennsylvania.

As I entered the 376 West Parkway that Friday, it was crowded but traffic was moving somewhat fast. I stayed in the far right lane—which some call the slower lane. I could see traffic up ahead as I was approaching the Squirrel Hill Tunnel going downhill at sixty miles per hour. I glanced in my rearview mirror for a split second and noticed a red pickup truck changing lanes every so often.

Thinking that just maybe he's late for an appointment or maybe heading for the airport, I was glad for the moment that he wasn't speeding in my lane. Suddenly, his lane started to slow down quickly like it does on the Parkway. He darted over into my lane.

He was going too fast on this crowded freeway, and I thought, "Why?" I felt uneasy, wondering if he would have time to stop if he needed to. Then, just like that, my

Thank You, Jesus!

lane started to slow down, too. By this time, he was right behind me.

Oh, my God, he's not slowing down. I couldn't see the truck's headlights. All I could see in my small Nissan Altima rearview mirror was the Chevy emblem in front. Then, it happened.

To avoid hitting me, he swerved off the highway pavement and onto the side of the road, brushing my rear bumper slightly. Off to the right he slid and quickly came back toward my right front fender. I felt a thud and for the second time, he shot off the roadway and onto the roadside, sliding some thirty or forty feet before coming to a stop. He jumped out of the truck, screaming, and heading toward my car. I had pulled off the road also.

"What's wrong with you?" he kept yelling. For a second, I was stunned. I almost got rear-ended, and this guy's waving his arms and yelling, "What's your problem? What's your problem?"

I was shaking like a leaf. My God, I could have been killed! I was afraid to get out of the car and look at my front right fender and door. He looked first and said, "Nothing's wrong. Nothing's wrong with your car, and you're not hurt either." Maybe not physically, but emotionally I was shook up.

I just sat in my car. Finally, I opened the door and got out, walking around my car and looked at my right front fender and door. Not a scratch, and yet I felt a bump and even heard a thud as his truck tried to come back onto the freeway. I didn't say a word. I headed back and got into my car. He just stood beside my car, and speaking loudly, said,

"You're not hurt, you're not hurt."

By this time, I had picked up my cell phone, dialed 911 and was talking to an operator. "This is 911. How can we help you?" I answered, "I need the State Police." A few seconds later, a voice said, "This is the Pennsylvania State Police. May I help you?"

I remember saying, "Officer, there's a man driving erratically on the Parkway, and he almost ran over me." The officer told me to get his plate number, and I told him that I had it. I repeated, "SP10145, red pickup, new." "What make is it?" the officer asked. I replied, "I'm not sure if it's a Ford or Chevy." Then the officer asked, "Are you hurt, sir?" Not sure, I replied, "Emotionally, yes." "Is your vehicle damaged?" "Can't say for sure, sir," I replied. "What's all that hollering?" the officer asked. I said, "It's the truck driver screaming that I caused this incident."

Then the officer said, "Mr. Totin, don't answer him." I was surprised that the officer knew my name. Then he said, "Mr. Totin, keep in touch with us if you need to. I just put out an all-points bulletin to intercept this red truck." I sat in the car awhile before I pulled out in order to calm down. Then the truck driver also calmed down and asked if I wanted his name and phone number. "Nope," I answered, "I have your plate number." Again, he asked, "Do you want my name and phone number?" and then gave it to me. I wrote it down, and he said again, "You're alright. Your car wasn't hit," and he drove off along the side because traffic was still backed up, moving at a snail's pace.

When I got home, I called my brother-in-law, George, and asked him to pray with me for peace and to thank the

Thank You, Jesus!

Lord that I was alright. I looked in the phone directory, and sure enough, there was the truck driver's name, address, and phone number.

Thinking back some twenty years prior to this time, I was given a word from the Lord that the devil was going to try to kill me. I chuckled, thinking, "Gee, it's a good feeling knowing God has been watching over me ever since." *He was there all the time* – a tune I hummed over and over.

CHAPTER TWENTY

All Things Are Possible With God

Many years ago, when I headed up the phone prayer lines at Cornerstone TeleVision in Wall, Pennsylvania, I received an early morning phone call from a man named Ralph. He said (and I quote), "Sir, would you please pray with me for peace?" I replied, "What is your problem?" He said, "The doctors are going to amputate my leg today in order for me to survive. I have cancer of the bone."

My heart was troubled with this request, and I asked, "Are they sure there is nothing they can do to save it?" "Yes," Ralph answered. "It was x-rayed last night just to be sure, so today's the big day." I asked Ralph, "How do you really feel about this?" Hesitantly, he said, "What else can I do?" I said, "Ralph, let's pray that God would change this diagnosis and stop the amputation and that they'll take one more x-ray this morning." I added, "Will you agree with me?" "You bet," Ralph said. So I prayed with him:

"Father, we need a Holy Ghost, blood-washed miracle in saving Ralph's leg. Lord, have the doctor's x-ray one more time even though they said they are already sure. Please, Lord, give Ralph favor, uncommon favor. In Jesus' name we pray. Amen."

Thank You, Jesus!

Ralph thanked me and said, "Okay, I'll let you know, Brother Steve." He hung up the phone.

I quietly prayed, "Father, spare his leg. Please. In Jesus' name. Amen."

Ralph asked the doctors, "Would you please x-ray my leg just before surgery?" There was no argument and an x-ray was taken. For whatever reason, the surgery was canceled and the doctor's said they'd treat him with medicine and therapy. Ralph called back rejoicing. God answers prayer. 11:59 p.m.

CHAPTER TWENTY-ONE

Cathy With A "C"

It was Saturday and, as was my custom since November 16, 2005, I was at my beloved Dorothy's grave. Placing a single red rose on top of the grave, I knew that my Dorothy was not there but with her beloved Lord and Savior Jesus Christ.

Parked at the backside of the cemetery was another vehicle, yet I saw no one nearby. The cemetery is surrounded by farmland and a large field. In the distance, I noticed a woman walking a very large dog which resembled a German shepherd. I continued to trim some grass and pull some weeds. Once or twice, I looked back over my shoulder, and I could still see the woman and the dog afar off.

Shortly after, I heard a soft voice break the silence once usually senses in a cemetery and looking up, I saw the woman of the field, next to the parked car, with the large dog. She said, "Sir, I didn't want to startle you with my dog." I jokingly said, "I sure hope I didn't startle him," since I was down on hands and knees.

Then, with her hand motioning to the gravestone, she asked, "Your wife?" "Yes," I replied, "My Dorothy, my love. Sure miss her." The woman said, "You loved her very much, but she's not in the grave. She's up there (pointing to heaven)." I smiled my approval.

Yep, Dorothy was probably looking down and saying, "Hey, hon, I'm okay. I'm happy. We're only separated for a season." I always try to find comfort in that remark. Sometimes I do, and sometimes I don't. I added that Dorothy was quite a loving person. She was in the ministry—an intercessor like Mother Teresa in Calcutta. Dorothy prayed for thousands of troubled souls for thirty-seven years. She sure knew how to touch God's heart, and folks received answers to their prayers.

Then, the woman added, "I was blessed by the inscription on the back of her stone." "Yes," I replied, "Dorothy had a dream a few years ago. One morning, she said to me, 'Hon, I had the strangest dream.' She saw her name in bold print and lit up - **DOROTHY TOTIN**. Then the letters started to rearrange themselves, and she saw these words created out of her name, **"INTO THY DOOR."** In the Bible, John 10:9 (NKJV) states, *"Jesus said, I am the Door."*

I started to tell her that Dorothy was a devoted Christian and very faithful to her Lord. Dorothy had a <u>personal relationship</u> with her God. Me? Well, I had religion, yep, religion for forty-one years, sad, so sad to say. Now, reading God's Word, the Bible, you must be "born again" spiritually and religion won't make it. No one goes into His Kingdom with only religion (see Romans 10:9-10 and John 3:3-21). If religion could get one into heaven, no one would need a Savior or someone to die in their place for their sins on a rugged cross as Jesus did. The Hitlers and dictators of this world all had a religion of their own choosing, but Jesus

Cathy With a "C"

wanted to reconcile man back to his Heavenly Father Who knew no sin but took our place and our sins on Himself on a cross of suffering.

"So, ma'am, one must be born again and only through Jesus, God's only begotten Son, can one receive eternal life in Paradise."

Then the lady said, "I want to be 'born again.' Can I?" After a pause, I responded, "Yes. Can I pray for you?" I held out my hand, and she began to tear up. Quietly, I led her in a prayer of salvation as she sobbed and prayed asking Jesus Christ to forgive her of all her sins and to come into her heart and change her. "Lord, I want a personal relationship with you like Steve has."

We ended our prayer, and she hugged me as she sobbed. I added, "Lord, baptize her in Your Holy Spirit and give her Your peace." Stepping back, she smiled, and I said, "This meeting is a divine appointment set up by God Himself." I asked her, "What's your name?" "Cathy with a 'C'", she replied. She thanked me, and as she was leaving, I handed her my first book, <u>*Help Me, God*</u>, and said, "It will be a comfort to you." As she backed away from me, I looked up toward heaven and said, "*Thank You, Jesus*. I'm blessed to share Your love with her, and she was so innocent; like a little child, she came to You."

I put my tools in the trunk of the car and said, "Hey, Dorothy, how about that? And you saw it all!"

I drove off smiling and thinking, "One more soul added to Your Kingdom."

CHAPTER TWENTY-TWO

He Will Never Leave You Nor Forsake You

[Hebrews 13:5]

It was the week of Christmas 2007. I was on vacation, when a staff member, Tom Hollis, called and told me that one of the Cornerstone TeleVision prayer partner's husband had passed away on December 18th. It was Bob Gulaskey. His wife, Priscilla, worked for me when I served as Phone Ministry Director in the 70's.

I was unable to attend the funeral, but when I came back to work in January, I called Priscilla to tell her I was sorry to learn of Bob's passing. I said, "If I can be of any help, please feel free to call." She thanked me, and I hung up.

On January 5th, I called Priscilla to see how she was doing, and she indicated that she was okay. Her three sons had just left to return to their homes out-of-state. I called her again in February, and we shared somewhat about our lives since she knew of Dorothy's passing in 2005.

I hadn't seen Priscilla for about ten years. She came to the station in the evenings to answer the prayer line phones, and I worked the day shift at the television station.

He Will Never Leave You Nor Forsake You

As we shared, I told her that if she ever felt she needed to talk to someone, she could call my office anytime and if she needed prayer, I was available.

One day, during one of our talks, I asked if she would like to have dinner with me perhaps, with Valentine's Day coming up, and since we were both without spouses. She accepted my offer.

Feeling I should do the right thing beforehand, I sent her a dozen white roses and a box of Sarris chocolates. I felt Bob would be pleased. I arrived at her home at noon and rang the doorbell. She opened the door, and we both were smiling when she remarked, "I've gotten older," and I answered, "Me, too." She invited me in for a moment, and I helped her with her coat then we left. On the way to the restaurant, she thanked me for the beautiful roses and box of chocolates. We were both a bit nervous since we'd both had long and happy marriages and hadn't had a date with anyone else for years. Dorothy and I were married 46 years, and Priscilla and Bob were married 49 years.

We entered Woody's Italian Restaurant in her area and enjoyed a great meal and talked. Hours later, we headed back to her home. I thanked her and said, "If you like, we can do this more often." She smiled and said, "Okay." I bid her goodbye and drove off, feeling pretty good about myself.

Ten minutes later, my cell phone rang. It was my daughter, Maria. I answered, "Hi, Maria." "Dad, I called your office and was told you left early. Where are you?" Oh, boy - it was then I realized that since November 11, 2005, I hadn't gone anywhere. No church socials; no singles group; only

Thank You, Jesus!

to work and church on Sunday. Maria broke the silence and said, "Dad, are you okay?" "Oh, yes, sure I am." Maria asked where I was, and I told her I was in Boston, a small town outside of McKeesport, Pennsylvania. "What are you doing there?" "Maria," I said, "I took a friend to lunch, an old friend I've known for years." I thought I could ease her curiosity and smooth it out like ministers sometimes do for a recent widow. "I don't understand," Maria said. I told her, "Her name is Priscilla Gulaskey. Her husband, Bob, passed away last year. We were friends." Maria's response? "Dad, I'm coming over to talk to you tonight." "Okay," I said, "What did you want in the first place?" "To thank you for the beautiful flowers you sent to my office." With her mom gone, I wanted to bless her, and I signed the card, 'Love, Mom & Dad.' I said, "You're welcome." "I'll see you later, Dad." And she hung up.

Oh, boy, after a great time with Priscilla, I wanted to say, *"Thank You, Jesus."* But now, I found myself saying, *"Help me, Lord!"*

Maria arrived, and I explained all about Priscilla and Bob's life together and our friendship. She seemed pleased. "Dad, be careful," she said as she hugged me and left. I dared not tell her about our future plans for more dinners.

Days went by, and I wanted to somehow bring these two ladies together - but how? I prayed and talked to my Heavenly Father about what to do. I didn't seem to get an answer.

Two weeks later, on a Saturday, I called Priscilla to ask if our Saturday date was still on. "Yes," she replied, "but first I'm going to a football scrimmage game between the

He Will Never Leave You Nor Forsake You

Pittsburgh Passions and the Baltimore Club, and women's football league. They're playing in my hometown of Elizabeth, Pennsylvania. You want to come?"

"No way," I said, "besides, it's 25 degrees outside." "Come before the fourth quarter ends then we can go to dinner." I said okay and told her I would see her later. I called Maria and asked if she was still coming over to balance my checking account. "Oh, Dad, I was going to call you. I can't because I'm on my way to watch a football game between the Pittsburgh Passions and Baltimore." My heart sank. Oh, no, I thought ... both at the same game.

So I told Maria, "Priscilla's going to the same game." "She is?" exclaimed Maria. "What does she look like?" I explained that she was about 5'5", 150 pounds, light brown hair, drives a white Buick Park Avenue with a soft, dark blue top. "Dad, I'll come Sunday and do your checking account." I told her that would be fine and said goodbye. When she hung up, I immediately called Priscilla. "Hey, guess what? Maria's coming to the game you're heading out to." "No way!" "Yes, she is." Priscilla asked what Maria looked like. I told her 5'0", 110 pounds, wavy light brown hair, and she drives a new silver BMW. I told her I was coming at halftime and to look for me. "Oh, Lord, I'll need You there for sure!" I took off, timing myself for halftime.

When I parked in the lot, a woman approached me and asked if I was Steve. "Yes, I am." "Come with me, and I'll get you in. Priscilla's waiting." When I got to her section, there were Maria and Priscilla, talking and laughing. You guessed it—they were standing side by side and talking to each other, not knowing that I was Maria's dad and Priscilla's friend all during the first half.

God did it His way. They both felt good about each other. Now, some would say that's a coincidence. Nope, that's God! All I could say was, *"Thank You, Jesus!"*

CHAPTER TWENTY-THREE

Perfect Love Casteth Out Fear

[1 John 4:18]

Two awesome mercies are embedded in this promise.

First, a Savior Who would come to *"save us from all our enemies."*

Second, the Savior would enable us to *"serve him without fear, in holiness and righteousness before him, all the days of our life."*

God spoke this promise from the beginning of the world, swearing it by a covenant to Abraham.

Someone reading this book needs a touch from Jesus. When the Lord ministered here on earth, He went about healing and restoring the afflicted by simply touching them. Jesus touched Peter's mother-in-law *"and the fever left her."* He touched the casket of a dead child and the boy came to life. He touched the eyes of the blind, and they could see. He touched the ear of a deaf man, and he could suddenly hear. Parents brought their children to Jesus *"that he should touch them."* His gentle touch changed everything. Multitudes brought their sick and infirm, and Jesus took time to reach out and touch them all ... and He healed them.

Jesus is waiting to touch you as He did Dorothy and me. Take time and find a place alone and just say:

"Jesus, I really don't know You personally. I know *of* You - will You be my Friend? I really need Your touch today."

"Jesus, please come into my heart. I know I haven't been a good person at times, but I'm really sorry. I feel so inadequate, so empty, so alone, so ashamed. Jesus, I know You are God's only begotten Son. Please forgive me and take over my life. Jesus, I need Your guidance and protection. Thank You for Your touch."

"I was told that You came to earth to reconcile mankind back to Your Father in heaven because of our sin. Jesus, I need a pardon, a full pardon. Thank You. In Jesus' name."

CLOSING

For The Moment

<u>Thank You, Jesus</u> is a book penned with no ending only because the miracles on these pages continue on.

Our greatest aim in writing our first book, <u>Help Me God</u> and now, <u>Thank You, Jesus</u> is to acknowledge our God and give Him all praise and honor for His unmerited grace in our personal walk with Him.

I have found it somewhat painful to recall testimonies of memories Dorothy and I experienced in *"Thank You, Jesus."*

My beloved was a beautiful, tender, warmhearted saint who knew how to touch the heart of God with her prayers. I was truly blessed to have her as my wife, lover, and friend for forty-six years.

Her love for her family and grandchildren, and her gift of the prayer of intercession for thirty-nine years, finally came to rest on November 11, 2005, at 5:18 p.m. with her Savior gently whispering - *Dorothy, it's time to come on home—I'm well-pleased with your dedication to my Gospel, good and faithful servant.*

At that moment, I was gently embracing her fragile

body of illness. Barely speaking, she whispered to me, "Hon, keep occupied 'til He comes," gently turned her head to her left and slipped into eternity with the One she loved so dearly - Jesus her Savior.

Therefore, my beloved brethren, be steadfast, immovable, always abounding in the work of the Lord, knowing that your labor is not in vain in the Lord.

(1 Corinthians 15:58 NKJV)

COMMENTS

It all started on a quiet Friday evening. My wife, Rosemary, and I went over to Steve's for the Friday night prayer meeting. There were a number of people there to praise and worship the Lord as always. I had been a Christian for a little over a year and was still a little leery of how to pray for people or to minister to someone. I just didn't know how to do it.

That night, as we went into prayer, there was a young woman that was thinking of having an abortion; she needed prayer. You guessed it. Steve said, "John, will you pray for her?" Well, my chin hit the floor, my mind went blank, and I wanted to leave. Steve took me out of my comfort zone. I went over to her, anointed her with oil, and began to say something. I still don't know what I said. However, I did the best I could do. God knew my heart.

The meeting ended that night when Dorothy, Steve's wife, came over and told me how good I had done. I was still shaking, wondering if I said the right words. I thank God for Dorothy speaking to me and encouraging me. Whoever went to the Friday night prayer meetings was blessed in one way or another. I was blessed by having Steve and Dorothy as such good friends; well, they were more than friends. They were like family. I thank God today for all they taught me through the years.

Thank You, Jesus!

Steve and I are still ministering together after thirty-one years of knowing each other; and it would never have happened if it hadn't been for the Friday night prayer meeting when Steve brought me out of my comfort zone as he did many others. It was a place of learning and hands laid on. Thank you, Steve and Dorothy.

By the way: the young woman didn't have the abortion!

John and Rosemary Hendrick

Dear Brother Steve,

After reading your book, *Help Me, God*, your book watered me in places that I did not know I was thirsty. Can't wait to read your second book.

Prisoner Greg, Angola, LA

Help Me, God was a delightful testimony of God's love and faithfulness, and God is truly an ever-present Help in our daily lives.

Worshipper Leslie, Bridgeville, PA

Your book impressed me as a reminder, no matter how touch times are, God is always there. Send me your new book.

Prisoner Ron B., Menard, IL

Thanks for sending me, *Help Me, God*. I loved the chapter, "Widow's Mite." Now, I have no excuse for not giving to God's ministries.

Inmate David B., Cresson, PA

Comments

Your book gave me strength to continue to trust Him and never give up. Thanks for thinking of me.

Inmate Robert, Loretto, PA

Help Me, God is refreshing and encouraging. That God's no respecter of persons even when we let Him down.

Housewife Treases, Lakeland, FL

Boy, that book, *Help Me, God* is an easy read. It reminded me of things I learned a long time ago. Looking forward to your next book.

Aunt Martha, Pittsburgh, PA

How many times I quoted your book's title, *Help Me, God*, and He did! Thanks for writing it.

Inmate Joe M., SCI, Fayette, PA

Your book is an uplifter. Thanks for being obedient. Do you have any others to send?

Retiree Dorothy, McKees Rocks, PA

Help Me, God is fantastic. Everyone should read it. I suffered from depression for years. It has changed me for the better.

CTVN Partner, Wichita, KS